Joints of Pain

Joints of PAIN

Living my Life with Rheumatoid Arthritis

Laura Pietro

Published by LAP Publishing
PO Box 471, Breckenridge, Colorado 80424

ISBN 0-9704186-0-4

LAP Publishing
PO Box 471, Breckenridge, CO 80424

Produced by Griffith Publishing
Printed in the United States of America

Table of Contents

PREFACE

My junior year in college I was required to take a course entitled "Family and Community Health." In this class, we read and discussed several books about chronic illnesses and other major health problems that people suffered through. My favorites were *Girl Interrupted*, by Susan Kaysen, and *Living in the Labyrinth,* by Diana Friel McGowin.

One author wrote about her mental disorder and the other was about a woman's struggles with Alzheimer's disease. These two books held a deep meaning for me as I read them. I was able to understand some of the feelings and thoughts that both woman were experiencing. In some small way I was able to feel what they were going through. And yet, through their own personal life struggles they were able to give others a look at their lives. They let people in to see what the world looks like through their eyes. I thought what a great thing this must be for individuals with the same prognosis as these authors faced. I wondered if there was a book out there by someone with rheumatoid arthritis. I searched at every big bookstore to see if there was such a thing. Unfortunately, I couldn't find what I was looking for.

That's when I decided to write my book. I wrote it because I felt it was important for others like me to have something to relate to. I want others to get a glimpse of what life is like with rheumatoid arthritis and give them more knowledge about the disease. As I began writing, I realized how therapeutic the process was. Things I had repressed started coming out as I typed away on my laptop. The word was out at last.

I thank everyone who has touched my life and made me aware of all the great things we have in this world.

They will all have a special place in my heart forever. I pass my courage along to those who haven't figured things out yet. Hold your head high and start making things happen for yourself. I have learned to cherish what it is I have and to be thankful for the experiences and memories I've made. Your life is what you make out of it, no matter what obstacles may lie in your way.

Introduction

About 43 million Americans have arthritis. This translates into approximately one person in every seven. Of that number, about five percent suffer from rheumatoid arthritis, the most severe form of the disease.

With rheumatoid arthritis, something unusual is happening in your joints. The white cells in your body, whose main function is to kill bacteria and viruses, also attack the collagen in your joints. Collagen is like glue that holds cartilage together. And cartilage, as we all know, lines our joints. When it is being attacked, the cartilage that makes our joints move smoothly becomes destroyed. The inflammation, pain, swelling and difficulty in movement are all problems associated with this condition.

I was first diagnosed with rheumatoid arthritis when I was fourteen years old. That's right, fourteen. Anyone with RA knows that it is possible to get it at even an earlier age than that. It is not just a disease for older people. When you are young and are diagnosed with having arthritis, it can be very confusing. For me it was difficult to understand that I had something that I imagined getting as I grew older. This book follows how I led my life before my diagnosis and after, and how I have had to make changes and adjust to my disease. The pages of this book contain my thoughts, my innermost feelings, and how I cope with the struggles I encounter.

I am writing this book for the millions of others experiencing life with a spider web of pain—a web we get caught in sometimes for days at a time and one that we are able to break through on sheer will strength alone to carry out our lives. I am also writing to let you know that I am scared. Scared of the unknown, the future, and how this disease will play a role in my life. I encourage you to find the strength and light that you have within yourself. Come be with me. You are not alone.

What is Rheumatoid Arthritis (RA)?

Rheumatoid arthritis is an inflammatory disease that is often more severe than other forms of arthritis. It is an auto-immune disease—a condition in which your immune system attacks parts of your own body. With rheumatoid arthritis, the synovial membrane that protects and lubricates joints becomes inflamed, causing pain and swelling.

If inflammation persists, chemicals are released into your joints that begin to digest cartilage, bone, tendons, and ligaments. The joint and surrounding muscles become weak. Eventually the joint may be destroyed.

Rheumatoid arthritis usually affects corresponding joints on both sides of your body. It can affect any joint, but wrists, knuckles and the small joints of the feet are among the most common sites.

Because your immune system is involved, rheumatoid arthritis can affect your whole body, including your heart, blood vessels, lungs and eyes. It frequently causes overall muscle aching and stiffness (especially in the morning), fatigue, anemia, and even low-grade fever.

The cause of rheumatoid arthritis is unknown. Some researchers suspect that it may be triggered by infection–possibly a virus or bacteria–in people with an inherited susceptibility. The infection causes immune cells (including white blood cells) to fight the invading organism. In the process, the cells attack the lining of joints as well.

1

My First 13 Years

As a little girl, I led a pretty normal life. I remember being rambunctious, full of energy, and always trying to match what my big brothers could do. I was born and raised in Southboro, Massachusetts. I have two older brothers—Dave, nine years older than I, and Matt, seven years older. I looked up to both of my brothers in every respect. Because of my great adoration of them, I was quick to do anything that was asked of me. When they were old enough to go in the swimming pool themselves, they would take me in, and when they got their licenses, they drove me around. I was always proud to be their younger sister and tried hard to follow in their big footsteps.

When my brothers went off to college, my life became much like that of an only child. I missed them greatly when they first moved away and tried my best to write a lot and keep in touch. When they came home for their short visits, their time seemed to be focused on being "adult-like" with my parents. At the time, I was too young and selfish to understand why they didn't focus on me any more. A few years of growing up took care of that, and we became closer than ever. They have both taught me a lot about everything they'd been through. My admiration still grows for them, for the love and support they have given me.

I lived in a big house with a great yard, a tennis court and swimming pool, and my parents gave me everything a growing child needs. They instilled in me a sense of responsibility and a strong set of morals, and have given me love and strength throughout the years. I grew up in a wonderful neighborhood filled with friends I still have to this day. I attended public schools known for their quality education.

In my younger years, I had a great passion for any creature God put here on earth. I remember my grandmother trying to convince me that toads would give me warts, but I couldn't believe that. There was a time when I had collected so many caterpillars in a bucket that they were crawling all over me, and one even crawled up my nose. There were always pets around the houses—a wonderful German shepherd named Max, some guinea pigs, rabbits, and cattle for my dad's hobby, raising cattle. There were always hurt and helpless creatures we found on the street or about the yard. The Pietro hospital was extremely accommodating with a cemetery in the back yard up on the hill for any poor little critter that didn't make it. I even had a horse, my dream animal, for a short period of time.

We had a fabulous garden where we grew our own vegetables, a swimming pool, a big yard accommodating any field of play, and lots of woods for exploring and seeking adventures. I remember finding hideouts and building forts with my best friend and neighbor Becky. Sometimes we would simply venture to someplace we'd never been or seen before.

I was somewhat of a tomboy. I preferred being outside getting messy to playing dress up. I would rather play with Tonka trucks than Barbie dolls. And I was no different at school either, always playing kickball with the boys and leaving the girls to play hopscotch on their own.

For the first thirteen years of my life, things were pretty smooth sailing. I have fantastic memories of my childhood years. I grew up next door to Becky, who was six months younger than I was. All through growing up she was the closest thing to a sister I ever had. We fought, of course, but we also had great fun together. Becky and I have memories, like most sisters do, that neither of us has ever shared with another. I definitely took the role of the pushy, bossy older sister, and at times I was extremely mean and a complete jerk. (Why do we do some of the things we do when we are children?) But when junior high came around, I must have reached some sort of maturity level that made me realize how much she meant to me.

When it came to my arthritis, Becky seemed to know how to deal with me better than others did. She didn't understand any more about the arthritis, but she understood a lot more about me. Maybe it was because her mom, my "Aunt" Sue, was there to help explain things to her, but I think it was probably that Becky just knew me. That's what sisters are all about. We have shared a very unique relationship throughout our entire lives. She now lives in Colorado, about three hours away from me. We try to get together as often as our jobs permit and we talk to each other as often as possible on the phone.

In the third grade, another dear friend, Martha, moved to New Hampshire. While we were friends, Martha and I shared endless laughter and had many good times and adventures together. After she moved away our parents helped us to keep in touch with one another and arranged for us to visit each other twice a year—once at her house and once at mine—for several years. She lived in a house that was over two hundred years old in Amherst, a quiet country town. I loved going up there to visit. It was so beautiful, and there were always many things we could do and explore. One time we went "frogging" barefoot in the pond down the street. Martha lost her balance and took a quick step to catch herself and stepped in a pile of cow manure. I'd never seen anyone flip out as much as she did at that very moment. Between the look on her face and the way she was shaking her leg, I had to hold myself from laughing so hard.

After the manure incident that day, Martha was ahead in frogs, 5-2, so I began getting a little desperate. Standing on a rock, poised and ready for action, I heard something move in the water below and instinctively swung my net in its direction. What I came up with was a catfish. I won the match, hands down, and we took the fish home to prove what we had caught.

Martha matured quicker than I did. We still wrote letters to each other for a bit, but eventually that faded away, too. Every now and then, I will catch wind of what she's doing which always brings me back to the times we shared together.

After Martha left, it seemed that none of the girls at school really cared to hang around with me—probably because I liked to play with boys so much, whether it was kickball, soccer, or baseball. When I tried to make friends with girls, I had a tough time. They told me I couldn't be part of "their" group. Sometimes they would taunt me for playing with the boys.

When I was in the fifth grade my teachers thought it would be best if I started going to a guidance counselor. I think I went once a week with two other girls I hoped to be friends with. Then two other girls who were new to our school began coming to the guidance sessions. One was

Michelle Vale, who became a close friend of mind. We came up with the phrase that properly suited one another—"bestest" friends.

She was told not to hang out with me by some of the other girls or she couldn't "be popular." Michelle wasn't caught up in that peer pressure trap, and we were great friends anyway. Michelle had a twin brother, Chris. For a while I had a crush on him, but over time Chris and I became more like brother and sister. We pestered and bothered each other, but as we matured so did our relationship. He was one of my closest friends in high school, but now I'm lucky if we talk once a year, let alone see each other. He's happily married, living in the Boston area.

Michelle referred me to my first steady baby-sitting job for a family that just moved into town. I was fourteen years old when I was introduced to the Littman-Quinn family. Now I am twenty-seven, and they have come out to Breckenridge for their last two February vacations to visit me and enjoy the snowy mountains here in Colorado. My relationship with that family holds a dear part of my heart. It is not often that a baby-sitter and family stick together that long.

I have watched all three of the Littman-Quinn children grow up. Jason was just turning two when I began and now is fifteen years old; Ryan was nine months old and is now thirteen years of age. I've known Anna since day one. As I'm writing this book she's now ten, and even though I went away to college when she was just one year old, we're still close. The Littman-Quinn family gave me a lot of inspiration into what I wanted to do for the rest of my life. Beth, the children's mom, has always been supportive of me. I so appreciate everything that family has done for me, including the advice, the endless opportunities and a chance to be as close with them as I am even to this day.

I remember talking to Beth at times about my arthritis. I was able to talk to her unlike anyone else in my life at the time. I shared some precious secrets of my own, and when I was afraid to ask anyone for advice, she'd be the one I ended up talking to. Even though I may never have had any extensive conversations with the Littman-Quinn children about my personal life, they were able to reach right into my inner soul and give me something very special of their own. They were and still are great kids or young adults, full of innocence and a longing to explore their world. I used to love watching how they grew and reacted to one another.

When Ryan was about three or four, he could put me into fits of laughter with his childish patter and imaginary games. I hold those unforgettable memories and hope to know the children when they are all adults and we can all laugh and smile about the times we've shared.

I baby-sat for a few other families as well. I could not get enough of kids, so I decided that working with children was what I wanted to pursue in college. I went to study Early Childhood because of the age bracket and my adoration for the younger years. The freshness and eagerness to begin learning is so intense with this age group. They are like growing sponges, sucking up every little bit you teach them and always looking for more. It's in these early stages of exploration that I feel it's important having the right person there to teach them. Somehow I put myself in that category and went to school for the degree and for my teacher's certification as well. To this day, I continue to take classes and courses on education and the early age group. I love attending conferences and workshops and never want to stop learning everything there is to know. My passion for children still burns strong, and I hope one day to open my own preschool.

2

Growing Pains

Junior High came around, and I continued to outdo even some of the boys in gym class. Fitness tests like sit-ups and push-ups were fun and challenging to me. I held the girls' record for some time in both sit-ups and pull-ups.

Halfway through the year something started going wrong. I can remember the first time that my wrists gave me a lot of pain. I was in gym class one day and we were all being timed at an obstacle/fitness course. It was meant to be fun and, for those of us who were competitive, a chance to really push ourselves. I jumped up to grab the first rung of a suspended ladder with no problem. In fact, my next few grasps were a piece of cake. When I reached for the fourth rung, I felt a sharp pain bolt through my wrist and immediately I let go and fell to the ground gasping in pain. I was embarrassed and tried to hide my tears from my friends and classmates who were looking on. For a few minutes the pain was intense, but eventually it faded away, almost as if it had never existed. I was excused from the course and sat in bewilderment as I watched everyone else continue.

That was my first memory of the pain I continued to have in both my wrist joints. They ached and bothered me here and there, and after a while I finally mentioned the pain to my mother. Knowing that I have a high tolerance for pain, my mother immediately brought it to my doctor's attention, who continued to pass it off as growing pains for another year and a half of my life.

I thought to myself that growing pains really sucked! And quite frankly, I was wondering why the rest of me wasn't hurting. After all, I was a growing adolescent. I played on a volleyball team that won the championship the beginning part of eighth grade, but all I could do was dig (both hands together underneath the ball)—with pain. It was also around this time that I took up tennis seriously. My goal was to be good enough to smoke my old man. When I was little, he had taught me how to play with two hands, and so I continued playing two-handed, even to this day. I probably would not have been able to play one handed. My wrists simply hurt too much. And those damn fitness tests. I could still outdo most of the others with the sit-ups, but I had to grin and bear it on the pull-ups and push-ups because they hurt so bad. I felt like a weakling. I could not understand what was happening to me.

After a year and a half of complaining about the pain in my wrists, my mother once again approached the doctor. I remember getting blood drawn for tests, but I wasn't exactly clear on what was going on. Perhaps my mom did try to explain to me that I was being tested for a rheumatoid factor, but what does that mean to an invincible fourteen-year-old? As a blooming adolescent, I had begun to pull away from my mother and can distinctly recall having selective hearing.

The day that I found out I had Juvenile Rheumatoid Arthritis (JRA), was a day filled with so many different kinds of emotions that I could not even deal with it, so I blocked it out. An adolescent is coping with enough as it was—and now arthritis? That's something older people get, so why were they trying to tell me I had it? And what was it anyway? Something that made you feel stiff and sore?

The immediate picture I had in my head was of an old man or woman bending over and walking with a cane. My first visits to the pediatric rheumatologists were nightmares to me. I had a lump in the back of my throat the entire time I was there. I wanted to cry out, scream, and let someone know that I was scared of what was going to happen to me. But the lump stayed in my throat for my first six-hour visit, and I carried on as if I wasn't even acknowledging that fact that I had this disease they all said I had.

I kept my answers as short as possible and never looked anyone in the eye. To compensate for my silence, my mother did most of the talking, which added to my frustration. She did this out of love and was trying to help me out the best she could. The more she tried to help me, the more I wanted to push her away. I know I wasn't speaking for myself, but how could she comprehend the things I was trying to sort out on my own?

By the time I was finally seen for that first visit, I was complaining of morning stiffness in my wrists, in my feet, and some pain in my shoulder and back as well. According to my medical records, I used to walk flat footed for the first few hours of the day until my joints would loosen up for me. Funny how I have a tendency to block out a lot of things from those times. As I look back at my records of my first visits the small details come back to my memory. I also find it very amusing as I read about my visit in July of 1987, that there are comments written about every joint they examined. After listing all the scientific terms about what was going on with my wrists and feet, the doctor wrote, "otherwise healthy."

There was also an occupational therapy analysis that states that my motion and movement was limited. My hand strength was weak for my age—no kidding!—so I was put on an exercise program including theraputty (like silly putty, only there was nothing silly about it) to help with my strengthening. Unfortunately, as an invincible 14-year-old, I didn't feel these would benefit me at all. In fact, the only time the putty came out was to capture some cool comics from the paper. I learned that the sticky substance could absorb ink and function as a rubber stamp. Although I never did my exercises, my strength increased slightly. I think it was the competitive side of me that helped me achieve progress. I would have my occupational therapist tell me what measurements of strength I had gotten last time and would muster up whatever it took to try and beat it. It was all a case of mind over matter.

Every four weeks I had to go back to the New England Medical Center with my mother, get tested for wrist movement and strength exercises, and asked the same questions I had barely answered the month before. The medication was the biggest adjustment of all for me. I'd never been much of a pill taker, but that was all to change. I first started on Zorprin®, an anti-inflammatory medicine, a time-released aspirin. Two in the morning and two at night. At the time I didn't realize it, but that dosage was the equivalent to twelve regular aspirin a day at age fourteen! They were bigger than anything I'd ever taken before, horse pills if you will. For the first few weeks I gagged a lot.

There were also peculiar side effects that needed to be watched for. For one thing, after taking my pills, I was supposed to watch and make sure that they did not go through my system and out my stool. Like I ever checked! And because of all the medication I was on, blood had to be drawn at every visit as well. I grew accustomed to counting the tubes they'd be filling up. I think ten was my record, including four of the huge purple ones. Oh yes, and peeing in a cup! As a 14-year-old, I hated doing this with a passion. What would my friends think? They wouldn't understand what this is all about. Heck, even I was still clueless.

If I paid attention when the doctor was talking to me and stopped thinking about how fast I could get out of there and how few words I could get away with, maybe I would have accepted it sooner. As far as I was concerned, it wasn't stopping me from doing anything I enjoyed in life. A little pain never hurt anyone, I told myself, and besides, I'd had whatever it was for the last year and a half and I'd gotten along okay.

After the fourth or fifth visit, my doctor was beginning to get concerned that I still wasn't dealing with my disease and doing what I had been told. She offered me the opportunity to see a psychologist. My initial reaction to this was to get up and leave, but the more I thought about it the more I accepted the idea. This would be an opportunity to speak to someone who knows roughly what I'm trying comprehend and deal with. Unfortunately, I was hesitant to speak, and before I said a word, my mother jumped right into the conversation to say that friends and family members were there for my support. What was she doing? I know she'd been pretty much answering for me up until this point, but I'd had enough.

My mother will never know how much love and anger I felt at the same time for her until she reads the pages of this book. She always seemed to communicate to the doctor that everything was just fine, but it was not. Not with me. Deep down inside, I needed help, but all that I ended up doing was repressing the emotions I was feeling and denying that this was something I was going to have to face probably for the rest of my life. I felt like there was no one who knew what I was going through.

I took every opportunity to brush the topic aside with my family. As for my friends, the few who knew, they thought better than to talk about it around me.

3

Repression

You know what happens when you repress things or try to act like they don't exist? I'll explain a few things that went on with me. From Day One, I began bad habits about taking care of myself. I took Zorprin (the aspirin) because I could feel a difference in pain level. It was only on rare occasions that I would miss it without feeling worse the next day. I continued to skip my strengthening exercises, only taking out the theraputty now and then to play with.

Amazingly, every other time I had a doctor's visit I would be tested for strength, and I actually had some gradual improvement over time, always falling within the normal range. My left hand became stronger than my right, but they attributed that to the amount of use because I am right handed. Maybe I got stronger because I kept playing tennis and doing other things that involved my hands. I usually skipped the exercises for motion. I couldn't be bothered with range of motion drills. Yet again, when I was tested, I did rather well, and the physical therapist, the only one I ever smiled at, would tell me what a great job that I was doing and to keep up the good work. I even eventually graduated from the green putty to blue. Just more toys that are still sitting around my old room in Massachusetts.

As other things in my life began to change because of my arthritis, I kept on trying to live my life the same. Soccer was part of my life, a sport I had been playing since I was in kindergarten. I was my team's star goalie. Unfortunately, a goalie with arthritic hands slowly becomes unable to block balls without serious pain. Routine catches and saves were painful sacrifices, but I made them until they became unbearable. I remember not being able to hold back a simple shot block that had never caused me problems before. I fell to the ground crying like a baby. I was taken out of the game. The coach wanted to put ice on it, which didn't make it feel any better.

I didn't know at the time, but ice is the worst thing you can put on an arthritis joint. It only continues the stiffening problem. No wonder my pain never went away. As a result, I sat on the sidelines for the remainder of the game. I felt like I had let my teammates down when we lost to the other, usually beatable, team.

Needless to say, my goalie days were over as well as my true passion for the sport of soccer. I still continued to play and enjoyed it, but it was never quite the same. Instead I became more serious in my tennis playing. Perhaps because I played with two hands, this was a sport that hadn't started hurting yet, or at least not enough to get me to stop.

Eventually I was excused from doing the push-ups and pull-ups of the fitness tests. It was like a degrading scene for me throughout high school. I used to be good at that stuff, but my disease had changed that. Soon I even sat out on volleyball gym days. Classmates who didn't understand made fun of me while I sat there and kept score. I wanted to be able to play. Days when I couldn't participate in any activities were tough. It was hard hearing, "Why doesn't she have to play?" or "Hey, what's your problem?"

If there were options in gym class and there was one activity I could do and one I couldn't, I'd get to choose first.

Many of my schoolmates thought that wasn't fair. They didn't know. In soccer practice one day someone kicked the ball straight at my left wrist. This never would have been a big deal before, but it was hit just right that I grabbed my wrist in pain and fought back the tears that puddled in my eyes. I had never felt pain so intense before. It's like having a migraine in your joint. In a few minutes the intensity wore off. All the other players looked at me dumbfounded. They didn't understand. Sometimes I think I didn't, either.

The visits to Boston became more frequent, about every month or so. In addition to the aspirin, they wanted to add another medication. It was supposedly something that would help stop the disease from spreading, in other words, put it into remission. For once I was interested in hearing what my doctors had to say. "Stop it," caught my attention and I was actually open minded about trying more pills.

The decision to begin taking Gold®, a remittive agent, was made in February of 1988. I had x-rays taken that day and based on the results the decision was made. "If the x-rays show an increase in erosive disease. . ." the medical experts said. Consequently the results stating that "X-rays reveal some progression of erosive disease in both hands and feet with new areas of erosions. Laura is a good candidate for Gold and we should advise starting soon, before she has functional disability."

Reading this now brings a familiar lump back into my throat. How naïve I was about myself and what was going on. With the Gold I was to watch for rash, diarrhea, changes in my urine, and mouth sores among other side effects. I remember thinking, "What the hell are they putting me on?" It sounded serious.

Within two weeks I developed sores on the inside of my lower lip. I had no rash, but was itchy and when I scratched, it produced welts that had lasted a couple of days. Needless to say, I stopped taking the Gold right away. What was next?

A few months went by after my allergic reaction died down, and my body rash and mouth sores went away. I started another hopeful drug, Penicillamine®. Three weeks went by and my body was tolerating it, so my dosage was increased. About the time I began this new medication, a teaching plan about the drug was reviewed with my mother and myself. I have absolutely no recollection of this, and only remember what some of the side effects were because they would ask me at every visit. "Any change in your stool? Mouth sores? Unusual itching?" (Yeah, an itching to get out of here!)

So Penicillamine it was, and for a while life went on back in Massachusetts. My feet were beginning to head on a destructive track of their own, and I was sent to be seen by a podiatrist to do an evaluation of my feet. My basic medical assessment started: "Patient with foot deformity (no kidding), splayed foot (made me sound like a duck), and prominent bunionettes (is this a food item?), symptomatic."

My own personal assessment: pain in feet = something wrong. At the time, nothing was done. Then it was back to the rheumatology department to have another assessment, this time by my occupational therapist. This test was designed to measure my upper extremity range of motion, activities of daily living and hand strength. The assessment went as follows: "Laura becomes anxious before coming to the clinic. (Do you think?) She is concerned with her progress in occupational therapy. She has done relatively well, however, and does not need to become so anxious and is aware of this fact."

I guess I always figured that if I did bad, they'd be onto me and know I wasn't doing my exercises.

My visits became more or less routine over the next few months. I would say I was fine, my mother would add her own comment, and they would write the same thing about me: "Well appearing, attractive teen, but subdued adolescent." At least they thought I was cute. The mouth sores came again, but would only last a night and were usually gone by morning. I stayed on the Penicillamine and they gradually stopped. Now and then I experienced minor flare-ups with additional pain and swelling. During these times, I took adult aspirin in the middle of the day along with my other meds. More drugs, my favorite thing. But it seemed to do the job for the time being.

X-rays on the following February in 1989, showed small improvements. It was relatively smooth sailing for me until my Zorprin began to go through into my stool. Complications with my feet worsened. It seemed to me that things were taking a downward direction. My immune system was pretty much non-existent. I caught every germ passing through. And I gained something new—exercise-induced asthma, which also acted up with my allergies. I was sent to get yet another assessment (can you tell I really enjoyed them?) by the pulmonary function laboratory for my lungs. The conclusion there: "Small lungs. Normal flows." That was the only assessment I actually enjoyed and learned from.

In March of 1990, I had my first encounter with finger trouble. It wasn't quite a "trigger finger" yet, but given a few more years would get there.

Due to some complications with the Penicillamine, which I cannot remember nor track down in my records, I was taken off it and onto Methotrexate in March of 1990. I began developing nodules not only in my feet, but also in my elbows, fingers and any other joint that I seemed to irritate. Despite that, my condition seemed to slowly be improving. My finger trouble temporarily subsided. Because my foot pain lingered, it was suggested that I try orthotics. This worked out great and lessened a lot of the pain I was experiencing.

Unfortunately, with every positive thing that was happening to me, an equally strong negative effect seemed to occur almost simultaneously. My right ankle was the next target. Before tennis matches I would have it taped. It became very weak and gave me a lot of pain.

Perhaps because of the increase in pain, another aspirin was prescribed and so *again* I switched to a new medication, Trilisate®. It wasn't long before I was having bad stomach aches that made me double over. For the two months that I was on it, my periods were completely irregular, something I had never experienced before. Needless to say, after this episode, I switched back to the Zorprin and felt better immediately. Besides that, Trilisate always left a bad taste in my mouth, though I was swallowing it.

I was aware of what I was taking. I was aware of the exercises I was supposed to be doing. I was aware of what was happening to my body. Nevertheless, not once did I feel or think that my arthritis was a significant part of my life. In some way I had convinced myself I didn't really have it. That one day I'd go to my doctor's appointment and they'd say, "Hey, you're fine!" Not that I was cured, but that they'd made a mistake. "Go ahead and continue with your life. We made a mistake!" That's what I wanted to hear, so that's what I heard.

But I was in denial. I never thought I'd be where I am today. During those years I never felt the darkness I feel today. I blocked out things I couldn't deal with things I wasn't ready to understand.

Looking back now, I think I would have been better off to have received help to cope with my disease. Maybe it could have aided in my understanding. Then again, maybe it would have sent me into further repression. In the end, it all works out. Sooner or (much) later, we change and grow and learn incredible things from and about ourselves. And the learning continues. . .

4

Good Times Remembered

Even with all of the physical problems my illness caused, my life throughout those years in high school were filled with friendships and memories I will hold onto forever. It was relatively easy not to think about my disease. Like a habit, you just take your disease for granted and accept the pain.

Everyone thought that I was a tough individual. I guess on the exterior, I was. Deep down inside there were problems and issues I had never resolved. I stored these negative things until my adult life when they would resurface to be dealt with. Even now, years later, thoughts come up that are hard for me to accept and cope with.

I went through my high school years like many other individuals. A few parties, lots of fantastic friends, and many memories. Most people didn't know that I had arthritis. I liked that because no one ever understood what rheumatoid arthritis was, including myself.

I went to the Christmas dances, Prom, and Ball, and was known for making my friends laugh. I was—and still am—fun to hang around. I was my own entertainment. I still crack myself up. I was also involved in lots of extra-curricular "stuff" such as the choir and jazz choir. I even auditioned and was selected my junior and senior years to participate in the district and all-state competition for singing. I played tennis and soccer all four years of high school and participated in a musical production.

I took my medications seriously enough that I didn't experiment with alcohol or drugs. I joined the STANDD (Students That Are Not Drinking and Drugging) committee. You had to interview and be chosen and we would go around to other schools in our towns and talk to younger students about the effects of alcohol, drugs, and peer pressure. We were role models. That involvement and the "drugs" that I was already taking managed to keep me out of trouble throughout my high school years. I had enough to deal with as it was.

I was fortunate to have a tight group of friends. Even though I never really talked to any of them about my arthritis, they all helped me in their own small way. If there were something I couldn't do, no one would hesitate to fix the situation before I would get embarrassed or ashamed of myself. For the most part, I kept up with everyone else, not letting anything stop me from doing the things I wanted to do. There are so many memories and experiences that I have shared with my friends and won't ever forget as long as I live. Because of them, my frustrations were cut to a minimum.

When I was with my friends, rheumatoid arthritis didn't pertain to me at all. Reality only came into view when I had to see the doctor.

I was a pretty good student, graduating in the top fifth of my class. I had my share of hard classes and my senior year I'd write my own "tardies" and go out to breakfast with my pals. For the most part, I was studious and cared greatly about how I did in school. That was another great thing about my closest friends. Everyone did well in school and took it somewhat seriously, but we still knew how to have a good time. I applied to colleges, got accepted by every one and remember graduation day well.

Part of me wanted to go far away from home, away from my parents and off to a new place. The University of Vermont was the farthest college to which I applied. I got accepted, but opted for the University of Rhode Island for financial reasons. I visited the campus with my mother and fell in love with the area. I would be right near the beach! It wasn't till college tennis competitions that I would get a chance to see what a beautiful place UVM was too. I was happy with my decision, and wasn't prepared to move so far away from home after all.

The day of my high school graduation marked the beginning of one of the best summers of my life. It wasn't one or two particular things that happened, but events that took place all summer long. It was the summer we were on TV for the fourth of July at the Esplanade in Boston. Every year, the Boston Pops Orchestra plays there. At night there are huge firework displays. We'd been going there for years and got there early so we'd have a spot in front and a chance to get on television. Someone every week was in charge of planning the fun we'd have on the weekends. We were very fortunate to have one another and be as close as we were. We laughed a lot, shared special memories, and kept each other out of trouble. (For the most part).

It was sad that fall when we all split and went our own separate ways to college. Seemed like we all went in opposite directions, everyone but my best friend Michelle. As it turned out, we went to the same college, the University of Rhode Island. And it was really no surprise when we chose the same major—Early Childhood Education. This worked out great for us, and we decided to be roommates. Our family members seemed to think it would be a big mistake, but it turned out to be one of the best decisions we could have made.

We lived together in the dorms for two years and in a house for one before we split and went our own ways for a bit. Michelle and I were totally typical freshman. We drank a lot that first year to catch up on all that experimenting we never did in high school, got OK grades, made it to most classes—and most parties. I remember we used to actually do shots of vodka and chase them with a Budweiser. Surprisingly enough, we didn't have that many sick nights. I suppose that was a good sign. At least we knew our alcoholic limits. We both always had silly crushes on guys in our dorms—Matt and Phil, the RAs everyone adored.

I spent the next four and a half years at the University of Rhode Island by the ocean. The beaches—such as Narragansett, Galilee, Scarborough, and Matunik—were incredibly alluring and beautiful. I love the water. And there were never any tourist crowds throughout the school year. I remember falling asleep at night to the sound of crashing waves outside my window.

Most of my classes the first year were standard required electives. Some were better than others, depending more or less on the subject matter and the professor. My eight o'clock classes were sometimes tough to get to, but I managed to pull through with decent grades. I also managed to be bold enough to try out for the Division I Varsity tennis team. I had spoken with the coach over the summer and had busted my butt to be in shape to get ready for try-outs. When I walked out that first day, I was slightly nervous, but all fired up and ready to play. It was a moment I had been waiting and preparing for all summer. I met the coach, Kate, and some of the other teammates who were returning members. Intimidating interactions were going on between the girls who already knew each other and had played with each other. And as it turned out, I was the only freshman there. I had nothing to lose. I hit against a girl, who played in the number four slot, I found out later. I found my groove and hit the ball with great concentration. The coach saw my skills and took me in as the seventh alternate player. The first year this meant I only played when someone was hurt or sick or when the other team happened to have a seventh player, too. But I made new friends, stayed in shape and improved my tennis game. Practices were sometimes intense, but almost always fun.

One of my greatest joys about those first two years on the tennis team was my coach, Kate. I looked up to her in so many ways. She always brought the best out of me. She had a type of arthritis in her hip joints. I can't recall what it was exactly, but she was the first person I ever shared real thoughts with about my own arthritis. I didn't say much, but enough for me to come out of my shell bit by bit and realize that there are people who understand or do their very best to understand. Kate and I occasionally shared stories with one another about how our arthritis made us feel physically and mentally. We discussed the effects of rain. She'll never know how inspirational she was for me. It may not have seemed like much, but when she told the team that she was retiring as a coach, my tears flowed. I am so thankful to Kate for the direction, the great times, all the laughs and her faith in my tennis game!

In addition to playing on the URI Women's Tennis Team and eventually being the captain my senior year, I was also on the Equestrian Team (horseback riding). It was only a club sport, but that is where I met some of my best friends. I have always carried a passion for horses since I was a little girl. Everywhere we went on family vacations, I begged to go on the pony or horseback ride. I can even remember my dad lying about my weight so I'd be able to ride both the pony and the horse. When I was in sixth grade, my father brought me to a riding stable where I took my first lesson on a big pony named Candy. I was lucky to take riding lessons for a year until it became too expensive. Unfortunately, I didn't start riding again steadily until my junior year in high school when I could afford it with my hard-earned babysitting money. I rode with a young instructor, Kathy, who took me trail riding, too.

At the University of Rhode Island I found out that the club team took all levels of riding, so I couldn't pass up the opportunity. What better way to do something I love, meet new people, and have the opportunity to travel to other schools?

For a while, it was a challenge to balance everything, including tennis, the equestrian team and, most important, my schoolwork. There were lots of trips, tournaments, and horse shows that sometimes required missing a class or two. In a way my busy schedule made me work harder, and believe it or not, I still had time to party every once in a while. As far as my arthritis goes, it really didn't even phase me at the time. I got the go-ahead from my doctor to visit every three months instead of once a month, provided I had my blood work done monthly. There were a lot of times I forgot or intentionally skipped my medicine. Nothing was bothering me much, and bad habits are hard to break.

Rainy days were all that would ever get to me. The label on the side of my prescription says to limit the consumption of alcohol, a rule I probably didn't follow as I should have.

I think the doctors attributed my healthier status to the Methotrexate® I was on. They kept asking me if I could feel a difference; did I feel better in general? Who knows? If I was ever hurting, I was probably ignoring it, but I never noticed a significant change in the way I felt. It could have been my high tolerance for pain, my adolescent ignorance or maybe it simply was no different. All I cared about was completing the four and a half years of school and figuring out what comes next. I continued to act like I didn't have this chronic disease.

The Methotrexate seemed to work well for me, and over time my doctors increased the dosage. In September of 1992, I reported feeling that I was in the best shape I'd ever been. My pain seemed minimal, and I was anxious to cut back on the amount Zorprin I was taking. At the time, I was taking five a day or the equivalent of 15 regular aspirin. I was happy when I was approved to only take three.

My feet, however, kept going off on a track of their own. In addition to the nodule already on the ball of my right foot, another nodule appeared. The toes in my right foot were continuing on their way to become hammertoes. A couple of months later, another small nodule showed up on the ball of my left foot, and more orthotics (molds fitted to the bottom of the foot) were recommended. Due to the destruction occurring in my feet, it was suggested to me that I stop my involvement in sports that used them. That would basically eliminate anything I enjoyed doing. I continued to play.

Breaking my hand in January of 1993 escalated my state of anger and frustration. On March 17, 1993 (Saint Patty's Day!) my medical report by my rheumatologist states, "I met with Laura at the request of the rheumatology team treating her for JRA. Physicians state Laura's mother had called asking for support related to Laura's emotional upset at this time. Laura reports knowing her mother called but feels she is able to discuss her problems with her brother who also has a chronic medical condition. Laura reports her recent feelings of emotional upset started when she broke her left hand, which has best range of motion. She reports frustration resulting from limitations to her many activities, i.e. tennis, horseback riding, and skiing. Laura states no current problems at school or with friends. She reports no suicidal feelings. Laura is youngest of three children, no significant family problems reported. She asked to meet again in three months during next clinic appointment. Assessment: Laura appears to be involved in age appropriate interests and activities with supportive intact family. Current stress seems to be related to long term adjustment to chronicity of her JRA. Problems: 1. Emotional stresses related to diagnosis and treatment. Plan: 1. Meet with Laura during clinic for ongoing supportive treatment related to adjustment to her JRA."

My first reaction to reading this was "Wow!" I had not realized that the lady I talked to that day knew exactly what was going through my head. I remember being reluctant to say anything, but it wasn't because I didn't want to speak. My mouth would not let out what my heart was desperately trying to say. Repression can be powerful. I was looking forward to meeting with this counselor again at my next visit. I knew that I was not saying much, but given time and patience, I would muster up the courage to break down the wall that was keeping me so silent. Unfortunately, and for unknown reasons to me, other visits never came. And so with that, my hopes of speaking to someone who would listen and understand faded away.

I did have my brother Matt, who has had awful kidney problems since birth. At age two he underwent two surgeries that saved his life. He too, has led his life always wondering what is going to happen in the years to follow. He has undergone several surgeries to cope with problems he has to live with for the rest of his life. We have shared feelings with one another on occasion about what things are like for us.

Of all people on earth, Matt may understand my thoughts, my prayers, and my inner battles better than anyone else.

5

Car Accident— Summer of '93

Before my next appointment with the doctor, another traumatic event took place in my life. It was the summer of 1993 and I had just gotten home after completing my sophomore year in college. Many of my high school friends came home for the summer, and we easily fell back into hanging out as a group. Four of us made plans to go to the drive-in movie theatre in Shrewsbury, Massachusetts. Walt Disney's *Aladdin* was playing, and we didn't want to pass it up. We knew the girl who sold tickets, so she'd always let my car in free.

We spent our time catching up on the year, watching the movie and after it was over decided to go back to someone's house.

I was the driver that night, and I pulled out of the theater in my 1984 black Mercury Cougar. I never did like that car. I hadn't driven more than 200 yards before a Camaro came out of nowhere spinning out of control and slammed directly into us. Fortunately, no one was seriously injured. I can remember seeing headlights coming towards us from a car that appeared to be out of control. My mind blacked out, and my next waking moment was of being pulled off the steering wheel. I looked around my car and knew exactly what had happened, that we were in an accident. The steering wheel was broken, there was glass everywhere from the driver's side window, the center console practically didn't exist anymore and my friends, all three, were gone. I asked where they were and was told they were all OK and sitting on the roadside curb next to the car. I could see them. I needed to know and see that they were all okay. As the paramedic was stabilizing my head with a neck brace and others were trying to remove the driver's side door to get me out, I looked at my lap to see a mix of glass and blood. I realized my face was bleeding pretty badly, and I couldn't see out of my left eye. I wondered if I had hit the windshield, but I knew I had put my seatbelt on.

My passenger Mike didn't have his seatbelt on and hit the windshield with his face. I should have made him put it on. Now it's a rule in my car. He braced himself against the dash, but broke it in two when his shoulder was thrown into it. Mike had forty plus stitches all over his face and needed follow up physical therapy for his shoulder. What had I done to my friend?

Michelle and Sara were in the back seat and ended up getting tossed across each other and landing on opposite seats. Michelle managed to get by with a few stitches, some bumps and bruises and the general trauma of being in an accident. Sara had a hairline fracture in her pelvic bone, was hospitalized for two days and had a tough time with her back.

Was it my fault? Not in any way, but that never stopped me from feeling guilty for being the driver. For a while I blamed myself for what had happened to my friends. According to Webster's dictionary an accident is "an undesirable or unfortunate happening that occurs unintentionally and usually results in injury, damage, or loss." But in my mind I kept thinking I could have prevented somehow.

I had sixty-three stitches in my face all around my left eye and lost a lot of eyelid tissue. Glass from the driver's side window, which shattered, embedded itself in my leg and arm, my rib cage was badly bruised from breaking the steering wheel, and I chipped my two front teeth. All these things, given time, healed quite nicely. Six months after the accident, I had to have a skin graph done to my left eyelid because of the tissue loss. I couldn't close my eye properly and had to put drops in it at night to keep my eyeball from drying out. The glass in my face, arm, and leg eventually worked its way out. A sealing bond was put on my teeth, and time took care of all the bumps and bruises, aches and pains. All except for one.

I returned to college my junior year with my confidence shaken. I felt like my face would never look or feel normal again. I have never been so self-conscious in my entire life. It seemed like every time I would go anywhere or finally head out to a party, someone always had to say or ask the wrong question. "What happened to your face?" or "What's up with your eye?"

I was so sensitive. It all hurt so much that I soon became a hermit and stayed at home. I'd rather stay at home and do my own thing. I had a new friend to hang out with; a kitten named "Toddler." I got Toddler the summer before I headed back to college and named her Toddler after my passion for children. I really wanted a dog, but it wasn't the right time in my life for one. I missed our old German shepherd, Max, and needed a pet companion. Max was always such my pal and a great listener too, a fountain of unconditional love, incredibly loyal and a big part of my life.

After the accident I longed for nights with Max to just cuddle and rest peacefully. I reached out to a kitten instead and she has been so great to me. Pets and their owners can develop unique bonds with one another that no one understands but you. Yes, she's older now, much lazier and because she is a feline, very independent, but we share a bond with one another. We've traveled together by car cross country and by plane. She probably has more frequent flyer miles than most of my friends. I know it seems silly, but she's my soul buddy. I missed her the summer I spent in Alaska, and felt lonely without her.

The year of the accident was also the year that I met my first serious boyfriend. In a lot of ways he helped me to restore my self-confidence. We were together for nearly two years. Eric was my first love, and I hold many fond memories of our relationship. He helped me get over the mental aspects of being in the car accident. However, my arthritis was another story. I don't know how much of what I was going through he comprehended, but I think he tried. I shared things with him that I'd never before shared with another. He seemed to read my thoughts and feelings before I could acknowledge them myself.

The car accident also sprouted arthritic activity throughout my body. I vaguely remember having stiffer days. In a way, it was a turning point for me. I realized that I could have died in the accident had I continued to go through the windshield, but I didn't. I could have lost my left eye, but I didn't. And I could have lost my friends. Experiencing something so traumatic really opens your eyes to the things you have and what's truly important to you.

I became more serious about my arthritis and even began to be more open about it. I made sure I took all the medication I was supposed to and even made a conscious effort to do the exercises I had been neglecting for the past six or so years. Better late than never.

That year my immune system was almost non-existent. I came down with bronchitis at least three times, including once with strep throat and mononucleosis. During spring semester my junior year I ended up having to drop a class and take two incompletes, which I finished over the summer. Bronchitis continued to plague me though the following years. Because I had asthma, whenever I seemed to catch a cough or the crud that was going around, I pretty much knew I'd get bronchitis. I'd always get antibiotics, more lovely pills to add to my collection.

A few months went by after the accident and six months since I had last spoken to the Social Work Services. We met again in September of 1993. Progress Note: "Met with Laura today individually for the ongoing supportive treatment related to her JRA and recent car accident requiring multiple sutures to her eyelid. Laura reports she will be returning to college this fall where her friends are very supportive. She expresses feeling lucky no one was seriously injured as she was driving and feels responsible for passengers although she was not at fault. Laura expresses feeling somewhat self-conscious about her injury but denies anger at this time. She expresses feeling anger at her mother who she feels worries too much about her. Also met individually with Mrs. Pietro to provide support related to car accident and Mom's belief that Laura needs additional counseling. Discussed Mom's reaction of fear and anxiety related to car accident and her daughter's safety. Also difficulty feeling overly protective of her daughter and son who also has chronic condition from childhood. Assessment: Family coping with understandable anxiety to recent car accident and Laura's chronic illness and relation to separation issue of adolescence. Plan: Continue to follow in clinic."

Upon seeing this woman the second time, I began to feel bitter towards her. I didn't understand why so much time went by before we met again. I was angered that it took my car accident to see her a second time. Of course, this was no fault of hers, but I distinctly remember not caring for any of the questions she was asking me or the prodding she was doing. I wanted to be able to say what I chose and not have to be drilled and asked the same questions five different ways just to see how I would respond. I never met with this woman again. And so with that went my hopes altogether. This was the one person I thought could help me, despite the fact that I was short with her on our two visits. I respected her, but didn't act that way at all. Instead, I closed up and tried to share nothing, scared to let down my wall. I could not let my feelings out.

6

Triggers

I remember the first time I woke up in the morning and had a finger that wouldn't straighten out. I was pushing it as hard as I could, with pain, and the sucker wouldn't budge. I even tried using my other hand to help. It wasn't until a couple of hours later, a hot shower, and about a million tries before it would finally reach its outstretched position. Anyone with rheumatoid arthritis has probably had this happen to them at some point or another. It's called a "trigger" finger. The finger can stick the other way too. I have fingers that are straight but can't seem to close into a fist. Others get crippled up into a hook that cannot be straightened out.

Sometimes the trigger seems to go away after a few days. Other times, it continues for months, getting worse until finally the doctor decides to give you a cortisone shot to relieve the stressed out joint. I had always heard that cortisone shots were pretty painful, but when you've had a trigger finger, it hardly feels like a pinch—and the relief in the joint after it's over is worth the pain.

Unfortunately, cortisone is not a cure for the arthritic joint, but merely temporary relief. I have had one finger shot three times now, maybe four. The trigger always seems to come back and haunt me. One doctor I was seeing in Boston even would have me wear a simple tongue depressor splint on the finger to support the straightening back out of the finger. Two or more shots at once can sometimes make driving home from your doctor's appointment very interesting. Your hands are practically numb which makes it hard to grip the steering wheel, especially if both hands have been injected. I had three done at once, two on one hand, and one on the other. Fortunately, Tiffany, a good friend of mine, had come with me and drove my car back to the mountains of Breckenridge.

When you wake up in the morning with a trigger finger, or two, or three, simple daily tasks become very difficult, frustrating and painful. Try washing your hair with a crippled hand. It's nearly impossible and extremely frustrating. You can't even hold a bar of soap without great difficulty. Your ten-minute shower turns into twenty, and the hot water doesn't help. You need to give yourself at least ten extra minutes to a get dressed because of the pain of pulling things on and buttoning them up. A day with a trigger finger is not a good day for wearing tight jeans, if you have them. Plan on struggling to open your car door and when you finally do, you will grimace when turning the key in the ignition. It's amazing the amount of energy that gets sucked out of you.

We take for granted all the things we do with our hands on a daily basis. We don't really notice until they can't perform like they have every other day in our life. It's then that you look at them and see the changes. They don't look like they used to. Your knuckles are bulging and hot. They are inflamed and severely swollen. You can hear and see joints popping and clicking when they're moved. They're not functioning normally. Joints start becoming deformed, crooked, and taking on a crippling look. They don't look like your hands anymore.

But we are human and through this all we make adjustments that are needed. We use our hands in different ways and hopefully learn to have more patience with ourselves. We fight back tears of pain and frustration and learn to do things other ways that are easier on us. We carry on with our everyday life.

Not only were my fingers beginning to trigger, but they were also falling out of line with their normal growth patterns. When I held my hands out straight in front of me, it was apparent that the thumb joint in each hand was more swollen than the others and sticking out in ways they weren't suppose to. To help this situation from getting worse, I was first given a splint for my left thumb and then my right.

They took a hot plastic mold and wrapped it around to hold my thumb in proper alignment. It was explained to me that surgery on my hands would be inevitable someday, but that this would slow down the process to that point. The splint made me crazy, and I couldn't wear it! I was told to wear it at nighttime and any other time my hands weren't in use. My hand ended up cramped in the morning after being in the same position all through the night. Was I defeating my purpose here? But instead of telling me I didn't have to wear it, which I hoped they would say, they ordered another one for my right hand. This one was made out of neoprene and included my wrist as well. When I had it on it forced my wrist to bend inward and my thumb to hang out. My hand and thumb were in alignment and opposition. Again, in the morning it took an hour to get my arm out of its position. The splints hurt, so I never wore them again. They are somewhere with my old silly putty collecting dust.

7

Career

As I've mentioned already, I have a great passion for children. Throughout my college years, I spent my summers in a few daycare centers working with children. My last two summers before I moved to Colorado I worked at a camp and child care center for children aged three to seven. My position was camp coordinator, and I got to do lots of planning and the majority of set up. The first summer I ran it was the first under new ownership and so I was given a clean slate to demonstrate my skills.

I absolutely loved student teaching the fall of 1995, my senior year. Needless to say, I was all fired up to put all that I had learned to work in the spring. After I graduated I went back to the child care center at camp and became the head teacher in a preschool room. They were having difficulty that school year holding onto staff members. Teachers were becoming burned out very quickly in that room. It was challenging, but all I could think about was how these poor children had already adjusted to four other teachers that year. I was there for two weeks when the girl I was working with gave her notice. It was a sad situation. I recruited my friend Tiffany to come to Massachusetts and fill the vacancy. She needed a change and so did these kids. And Tiffany, I knew, was wonderful with children.

The rest of the school year went great. I put together a graduation ceremony, including playing a videotape in the background showing the children doing classroom activities. I made a folder on each individual child dating back to January when I had started with them. It wasn't much, but I made the commitment that they needed and the children needed. I kept my plans to move to Colorado, but my positive experience reassured me that I had done the right thing with my education. By the end of the six months, the children and I grew close, and I developed wonderful relationships and made great breakthroughs with a few of them. It was hard to say good-bye and know that I wasn't even going to be nearby to visit them.

During this six-month period the first falling out I had ever had with my arthritis occurred. I was seeing an adult rheumatologist at the New England Medical Center in Boston, and I began having complications with Zorprin. It was passing through me on a consistent basis and therefore wasn't being absorbed by my system. This caused me more pain and inflammation. Perhaps it was due to everything that I was going through, my first exposure to the real world after college. I was incredibly busy not only as a preschool teacher, but was holding down a night job at a retail store as well. With my plans to move to Colorado, I wanted my bills paid off so I could have a fresh start for when I got there. Since Zorprin wasn't working for me, whether or not the problem was caused by stress, a decision was made to try Naprosyn®.

I was on this drug for approximately three months. Those months were filled with painful mornings and stiffness in more joints than I knew I had. My hips hurt, my knees creaked, and my feet were unbearably painful. Sometimes I could hardly walk. I couldn't use my hands to wash my hair in the shower or button my clothes or sometimes even start my car. The doctor eventually switched my medication to Voltaren®. This drug was even worse. I remember waking one morning to go to work, and my body wouldn't function. Everything hurt. It felt like my disease was eating away at me. My whole body was collapsing. I was in pain whether I moved or stayed still. A hot shower did nothing. It was my first real taste on how badly my rheumatoid arthritis was affecting me.

About then my mom walked into my apartment I lived in attached to the back of their house, where my grandparents had lived when I was younger. All I could do was collapse in her arms and cry. I tried to go to work. I thought of the children.

When I finally got to the school, I was unable to put my pain and feelings aside and wanted to scream out. I was able to go home and spent the rest of the day in a miserable silence curled up on the couch. I called my doctor and went back to the Zorprin, which I felt great comfort in. Maybe my body wasn't absorbing it all, but it was 100 times better than what I had been put through. By May, things were essentially back to normal for me and I could go on with my plans to move out West.

In June of 1996, Tiffany and I moved out to Breckenridge, Colorado. We already had found a place to live, so our priority became finding jobs. I ended up getting a job as a one-year-old teacher at Carriage House, a child care center in town. This facility served infants aged two months through six years. The center itself was divided into three different sections for programs appropriate to age groups.

Mountain Top Kids was the toddler program, which was further divided into infant, one-year-old, and two-year-old rooms. When they graduated from the Mountain Top, they moved to Discovery Kids, the preschool room for three- and four-year-olds. Finally, they proceeded to Breck Kids, the kindergarten enrichment program for those preparing for and already attending kindergarten. Although I would have preferred an older age, I was happy to work with younger kids, and I enjoyed the people that I met and worked with. I had the opportunity of working with a guy named Bob, who was fabulous with the children. He once drew a house with a tree in the yard on the bottom of the wall in our room to help one child get over her fear of spiders. Once she realized that "Sammy the Spider" had a home too, the girl's fear gradually went away. We had a great partnership in that room. Bob was young, full of energy, and a terrific person to work with. Together we made the room fun.

I stayed in that room for a year and took a class in Administration at the local community college. It was the only course I needed for my director's certification.

Working at the Carriage House gave me the experience I still needed. Unfortunately, it also started to take a toll on my body. When working with one- and two-year-olds, you hold at least 40 to 50 children a day. You pick them up for diaper changing, when they're sad, when they've been hurt, or when they just want some loving. There is almost always a little one in your arms.

My shoulders began feeling the strain of picking up these little people all day long, every day. My joints began to weaken, and the wear and tear of arthritis set in. Bob would put children up on the changing table so I wouldn't have to lift them. He carried with him a genuine concern and curiosity, asking questions about my arthritis and, for the first time, I didn't mind explaining it to someone. He truly cared and was always trying to make things easier on me.

After a year in this program, I decided to move on. There was a position open in the kindergarten enrichment program in the same building, so I approached my directors and explained to them my situation. Everyone was already aware of my disease and realized that it was a matter of time before I needed to work with older groups.

Another woman working in the infant/toddler program also had rheumatoid arthritis. Until then I had not met anyone, aside from those I'd seen in the clinic, suffering from the same disease. She worked in the infant room and was to turning fifty that year. She looked more as if she was seventy years old. Barbara grew up in Colorado and had been diagnosed for a number of years. She was taking no medication and was so stubborn that she wouldn't even see a doctor about it. She had high blood pressure and was slightly diabetic, but refused to take medications for those conditions.

Barbara and I had many conversations about what arthritis puts a person through, and she opened my eyes to what I could be like in 25 years if I didn't take control. I talked to her several times about trying to get medication that might help her, but her mind was set and nothing was going to change it.

I got the position in the kindergarten enrichment program and moved over to the Breck Kids room. I was excited to work with this age group again and the people I worked with there were great. The summer was packed with fun. We took the children on field trips into Denver and every week there was soccer, tennis, swimming, roller blading, mountain biking, and many more activities for the children.

Every Wednesday was Beach Day and the children would take turns selling lemonade to help raise money for our non-profit organization.

When the opportunity came to be assistant manager at the Children's Center for Breckenridge Resort, it was tough for me to leave the Carriage Center. I had become acquainted with most of the parents and loved the children and my co-workers dearly. However, this was a chance to take another step in my career, and to learn the operations side of things. The manager knew me from the administration class we had taken together and was the one who told me about the job opening for the winter season of 1997 and 1998.

I was interviewed and accepted the position. That September I brought all my enthusiasm to the job. The center was open seven days a week and every holiday. Kristin, my manager and mentor, and I managed a staff for two children's centers with a total of 150 employees. The more I learned, the more I enjoyed my job. I held this position for three seasons. One summer I spent in Alaska and one in my hometown, Southboro, Massachusetts.

I decided to make another move in my life. Although my years as a manager have been great and I can't help but know the experience will help me with my future, I missed the children. I longed to interact with them as their teacher and not just be someone who's always passing through the room. My goal is to teach. Though I'd love to teach kindergarten (my favorite age) my certification is extends from kindergarten through Grade 3.

8

Shots

When I first found out that I would be taking methotrexate as a shot and not orally, it was good news. It would certainly mean no more awful stomach aches that led to restless nights of sleep. In addition, the shots would mean eight fewer pills to take each week.

As a little girl I had bad allergies that required an allergy shot once a month in the arm. So I figured it would be a piece of cake. Although I was anxious, I wanted to learn how to do the injections myself. Anything was better than drinking eight ounces of water to get down about a dozen pills before bedtime.

A friend of mine, Linda, was a nurse and sweet enough to help me. She talked me through my first few shots. The shot itself did not hurt, but immediately following it the injection sight was slightly sore for a few hours. I learned how to do the shots myself and actually did not mind it. The toughest thing about it was that since the shots were intramuscular, it was extremely important to not inject into a vein.

When the needle is first in place, you pull back the plunger slightly to assure there is no blood in it. No blood, no vein, and you're all set to go. If there's blood in the needle, that leads to complications. About my fourth or fifth solo shot, I pulled the needle out too quickly, and it bled for about a minute. I panicked, thinking I had accidentally injected my vein instead of muscle. I called Linda and told her what had happened. I was prepared to learn that, with my luck, I had really messed things up.

Everything was fine, but from that incident on I felt sick to my stomach when it came to the shots. I had scared myself, and the amount of blood I shed those few minutes was alarming to me, especially since it was from a measly shot. From then on, everything about the shots made me feel queasy. From the smell of the alcoholic swab, doing the shot itself, to seeing my blood come out, I became ill. The shots themselves were not so bad, but I always got that sick feeling again. Doing my own injections quickly became something that I didn't want any part of.

I was soon wishing I had the pills to take. Psychologically, the shots were making my stomach feel the same aches and pains I'd experienced with the pills. Either way, I lost.

Here is my understanding and interpretation of the way Methotrexate works. It takes six months in your system before it can begin working. It may put rheumatoid arthritis into remission any time after that, or it may take a lifetime. I had been on oral Methotrexate for years, eight to be exact, and I never once noticed any significant difference. In fact, in my opinion, things had gotten worse in the last couple of years. Had I continued to take it, my arthritis may have gone into remission. Or perhaps it would have never worked out for me. So do I just keep taking it, get used to the stomach aches, grin and bear it, and hope forever?

I did not make it that far. I dreaded every Wednesday, "shot day," when I was supposed to inject myself. I think that if I had felt the medicine made a difference in my condition it would have been a different story, and I probably would have kept up with them. But the thought of taking these shots for the rest of my life was completely unappealing to me. I couldn't bear the thought. I stopped intermittently and then for good the summer I went to Alaska.

9

Feet

My disease affected my feet as well. When this began happening, I realized that my whole body was being attacked by this disease and not just my wrists where it was first diagnosed.

My bones along the little toes grew outwards giving my feet the appearance of having bunions. It looked as if I had webbed feet, like a duck's. Over time, the toes in my right foot began to hammer up (curl up), and I had a bump on the ball of my foot that kept getting bigger and bigger every year. No surprise, but the bigger it got the more pain I had. I had been seen by podiatrists, but none of them had solutions for me other than to stop the things I enjoyed doing with my life. Somehow, I was told, if I didn't use my feet again, they would be OK. I was not prepared to stop using my feet.

Early on it was strongly suggested that I should stop playing soccer and tennis because those activities would make my feet worse. Quit doing the things I loved that kept me going in my life?

I was told that foot surgery was probably inevitable and that my feet would never be the same. These were my options. Option 1 would be to stop the sports, be miserable, as I saw it, and eventually my feet would still need surgery. This was not very appetizing to me, and I ruled out that absurd option right away.

My second option was to continue to play and enjoy what I could before it was too late. Someday I'd need surgery, but that was okay. This choice made the most sense to me, so I continued on doing and playing whatever it was I wanted to do. I had pain, but I felt it was worth it. I still feel it was worth it. I was having fun and not missing out on things I enjoyed doing in life. No matter what the pain may be, I don't ever want to stop being active in my life.

As time went by my feet got worse. After eight years they were horrendous. After living in Breckenridge for nearly two years my feet worsened. Skiing, tennis, hiking, biking, and most other activities sped up the process, but I wouldn't trade in any one of those days if I could.

On the slopes I could make only two or three runs before my feet would hurt so badly that I would run inside and yank my boots off. Running always bothered my feet, but before long mountain biking, roller blading, and sad to say sometimes just simply walking, also hurt. I began to notice I wasn't walking quite right to compensate for the bumps on the bottoms of my feet.

I decided entirely on my own that something had to be done. It was time to go see an orthopedist. Was surgery an option to rid this misery? Had I screwed things up? What would the end results entail? I had questions and wanted answers! This couldn't go on!

My rheumatologist in Denver recommended a few orthopedic surgeons to me. He had already done his own analysis of my feet and talked about the possibilities of surgery. It was the first time I had heard anyone talk about the procedure and say that the results were fairly good. Perhaps the eight years had been an advantage. Apparently throughout the years, the techniques had improved, and the success rate for the type of surgery I required was better than any hip or knee replacement doctors had ever done.

I was recommended to some of the best orthopedic surgeons in the West. Very encouraging! Everything sounded great. I was hoping to have new feet for 1998.

I called immediately and made an appointment to get an official analysis of my feet and my surgical options. Technically speaking, I had already made up my mind and was ready to do it. All I needed was a surgeon and a date. Dr. David Hahn with the Denver Orthopedic Specialists said he could fix me up in no time. We set a date for February 17, 1998, and I anxiously waited for that day to come.

It seemed odd to me that when surgery was first mentioned in years past, I would flip out on my doctors. How could they ever think that I would need surgery? I sincerely doubted that it would ever get that bad. I knew that things doctors say may happen sometimes don't. Now I welcomed the thought of surgery and new feet. I couldn't wait. I was tired of the pain my feet were putting me through on a daily basis.

Without a sturdy foundation the whole building will fall down. That's exactly what was happening to me. I talked extensively with Dr. Hahn about the procedure he would do and what kind of results there would be.

The procedure was called a Clayton Hoffman's procedure and went something like this. The bone on my left foot was shaved on the outside. (No more duck action.) With a small incision, the surgeon removed fluid and built-up cartilage and shaved part of the bone away. The misshapen bone had limited my shoe selection since adolescence and had grown quite painful.

On the right foot, two incisions were made—one between the second and third toe and another between the fourth and fifth toe. A small portion of each toe joint, with the exception of my big toe, was cut out and removed. Because all the smaller toes had hammered up, they needed to be straightened out. Ligaments and tendons were torn and cut to accomplish this and then metal posts were placed through the ends of my toes to hold them in place over the next few weeks. Extra tissue and fluid that was causing the bump on the ball of my foot was also extracted and then the bone on the side of the foot was shaved.

I had crutches, but those first couple of days I attribute getting around to Jeff, my boyfriend at the time, and Tiffany, my good friend. Without their support, I would have had a rough couple of weeks. The road to recovery was pretty quick, at least quicker than I had anticipated. I was up on crutches without assistance within three days.

As the days went by, I found I could put more and more weight on my left foot and finally some weight on my right heel. After three weeks the posts came out. These pieces of metal were four to five inches long with little knobs on the ends. They just needed a little tugging, and out they came. The procedure turned my stomach slightly, but was over before I knew it.

I was happy I had waited until after my appointment to eat lunch. My foot was still looking pretty funky, but because the swelling was down enough they put a walking cast on. That meant no more crutches and also that I could try to begin walking normally on the foot again. The cast went up to just below my knee and down beyond all of my toes. I chose my favorite color, blue, for my cast.

It was my first cast, so I had it signed by all my friends. Two weeks later, I was a free woman with new bionic feet. Well, almost. I limped a little at first, but eventually threw a pair of ski boots on and hit the slopes. I was still tender and took only a couple of runs before putting the boots away until the following season.

It was a strange feeling having "new" feet at first. I didn't realize how much my walking had changed to compensate for the bump on the bottom of my feet. I felt like I was learning how to walk all over again. I gradually got back into the swing of things. Some hiking here, a little biking there, and I still had times and days of soreness and tenderness, but that got better every day. Shoes were not as much of a problem like they were before. The ones I had fit me so much better and I could walk barefoot once again! I was even able to wear women's shoes, something I never could do before.

As time goes on, the same procedure will have to be done on my left foot. Only two years later after the surgery, I could already feel a bump beginning to form on the ball of my left foot. My toes have hinted to me that they, too, will eventually hammer up. I will cross that bridge when the time comes and do what needs to be done.

10

Summer of '98— Alaska, the Last Frontier

I had always had an urge to travel to Alaska and live in America's last frontier, so when the opportunity presented itself, I had no choice but to go. What better way to get there than to take a road trip! My boyfriend Jeff and I both got jobs in Denali National Park. He was a raft guide on the Nenana River for a rafting company, and I worked in a gift shop. It was the first time in my life that I called myself a bum. Even though I was a MOD (manager on duty) I still got minimum wage. I met a lot of great people. We made some new friends and got to experience the beauty of Alaska one of the treasures on this planet.

In the two weeks that it took us to get to Alaska, Jeff and I managed to visit seven other national parks and camped out every night except for one. At first I was a little concerned about how much camping, especially sleeping, my body would take. At times I'd been camping and had absolutely no problems with my arthritis at all and slept like a champ. Other times I'd been miserable and stiff after a few nights on the ground, hating myself for loving the great outdoors. Fortunately, we had great weather throughout the trip. It got cold at night sometimes, but we had a good set-up in the tent, so I managed without incident. I brought my fiber bed along for Alaska (I don't leave home without it), and put it in the tent every night under our sleeping bags. Since I brought my down comforter too, we threw it on top, and we were warm and snug. We called it "cush palace," it was so cozy. Car camping is a great thing, I decided.

Once in Alaska it was nice to sleep in a bed, but my body withstood the two weeks of travel just fine. From there on things got worse. Despite the fact that I had a comfortable bed, my bad days began to outnumber the good ones, and I became aware of my deterioration. Perhaps it was the weather, or maybe it was triggered by changes in my life. Jeff and I ended our relationship as soon as we got to Alaska, and there were days I struggled with the after-effects of that experience and found myself extremely frustrated.

Jeff had been a special person to me—still is, and always will be. We had a lot in common and became really close friends. We enjoyed doing the same things and hung out together. We made each other laugh. We took things as they happened day by day until we eventually took our relationship to an intimate level. I think that Jeff and I were better off just being friends, but I thoroughly enjoyed the times we spent together and the opportunity I had to go to Alaska with someone.

Our relationship ended by mutual agreement, and it was definitely for the best. Still, it was hard for me because I'd wanted so much to maintain our friendship. Jeff had helped me through some really tough times with my foot surgery, and for that alone I will always be grateful to him. Now that time has passed and we have both moved on with our lives, we have been able to become friends once again.

After my foot surgery I did not get myself into any kind of workout routine. It just seemed impossible. Any length of time up and about on my feet sent my "dogs" barking. I used to be able to just hop on my bike and ride. Occasionally my hands would ache for a while afterwards, but nothing substantial. My right foot would get sore, but not for long. That summer my shoulders were worse. Sometimes when I woke up in the morning, I couldn't raise my arms above my head or pick things up, much less sit hunched over my bike for a simple ride. If I wasn't hurting before I went on a ride, I certainly felt it by the end of my excursion.

I remember riding my bike down the main highway between Fairbanks and Anchorage. I thought about all the times I'd ridden my bike. I even recalled memories of my first pink Schwinn with a banana seat and all. I saw a moose on that bike ride, right on the side of the road. We stared at each other for about a minute before he rambled through the thick tundra. For a fleeting moment, I forgot my pain.

Sometimes I went to bed at night motivated to get up early the next morning, springing to my feet and doing something before it was time to go to work. When morning time rolled around, however, I couldn't turn my neck from side to side. Instead of leaping out of bed, I limped across the street to use the bathroom. Even to sit down and work on this book hurt me some mornings. I'd wake up having two trigger fingers and stiff shoulders, wrists and neck. Even walking to breakfast was a chore. I couldn't help but complain to my roommate as we strolled to the dining hall. I wondered aloud if the Zorprin I took the night before had made its way through my system without absorption. It seemed to happen quite often, but I knew that when I'd tried to switch to other pain medications nothing worked as well as the Zorprin. I couldn't win.

Despite my troubles with my arthritis in Alaska, I remember good times I had when I was there. With twelve other friends and acquaintances, I rafted the longest stretch of white water in North America on the Talkeetna River. On this three-day trip, I saw salmon the size of sharks, about a dozen bald eagles flying freely through the air, and even a black bear. In Denali National Park, I saw hundreds of beautiful wildflowers, caribou, grizzly bears, wolves, other wildlife, and stood face to face with the tallest peak in North America, Mount McKinley, 20,320 feet high—a breathtaking sight. It occurred to me that my body might get so bad, that I might never witness these miracles of nature again.

11

Pain

Whether physical, emotional, psychological, or spiritual, every person on earth suffers pain. The degree of pain from individual to individual may vary, but we all have pain. It's part of being alive, part of being human, and is part of who we are. Pain is inevitable. But don't feel like you haven't a choice, because you do. How you decide to cope and deal with the pain you're experiencing is your choice.

I try so hard to be tough sometimes that I end up feeling the complete opposite. The shots were not that bad—not at first, anyway. Sometimes I think about the pain that others have, people who suffer far more than I do.

I don't like it when people feel sorry for me. When people ask me about my disease, I don't mind telling them, but the last thing I am trying to accomplish is for them to feel "sorry" for me. I have a great life, and I continue to do almost everything that I want to do. Sometimes I need to make adjustments. Don't we all?

In my times of toughness and days when I can't seem to feel strong, I sometimes break down and cry. I grow tired of it all. Tired of taking medication day after day; tired of hurting in the morning so bad that sometimes I have difficulty dressing myself; tired of going to the doctors, every two or three months; tired of the blood tests, the ongoing lab work. The hardest thing to get through, I suppose, is the stiffness and pain, especially when it prevents me from carrying on ordinary everyday details of living.

On days of severe pain I sometimes get depressed. I have read books on arthritis and have learned that many people suffering from this disease frequently have depression. I am thankful for not having a depressive personality. I'm generally a happy-go-lucky person, but there are times when I feel like I've hit rock bottom and it seems impossible to get back up again. I lose my motivation to do anything, because everything hurts so much. Unfortunately, doing nothing makes things worse. Nothing gets loosened up except the stir of emotions. The frustration and aggravation that overcome me can be intense.

I begin to think to myself, "Is there anything I can do so I won't feel like this anymore?"

There has to be something, I think. I see the doctor, I take my medication, do the lab work, but that's not enough. I am cautious about eating certain foods, I watch my diet and try to exercise regularly.

There are times I don't want to go to bed at night because I know how I'll feel in the morning. It won't matter how much medicine I take or what position I sleep in or what I sleep on. It is going to be a day of suffering and pain.

Then the day comes on me, and it's just as I knew it would be. Some days it gets the best of me, and all I can do is struggle through the bottomless pit and try to scramble my way back to the top. I've cried out of frustration. I've shed tears because I wasn't able to understand what is happening to me. Even so, I always manage to live to see another day.

Other times I mull through the day, doing everything in my power to ignore the pain I'm in and busying myself to keep my mind off of it. If I don't try at all, it seems to lead to defeat. I know I have got to keep my head high and know my limits. As difficult as it is for me to say this, my advice to anyone afflicted with a painful condition is to know yourself and what your pain is capable of doing to you before it grows worse. The situation will only worsen if you push yourself beyond the pain you already withstand. My stubbornness in years past used to get the better of me, but now I know better what my limits are. This has been a milestone in my maturity.

For anyone in constant pain, your most important need is your need to rest. The fatigue that accompanies rheumatoid arthritis can be sometimes intense. There are days when it's hard to get out of bed. Pain can suck the life and energy out of you. Everyone suffers from pain at some time or another in their life. Some suffer more than others and all have different ways of coping. Some days we're incapable of coping. Some days a hot shower, plenty of rest, and additional pain medicine cannot even take the edge off. Fingers are stuck, shoulders can't be raised and your steps are crippled from a combination of your feet, ankles, knees, and hips.

The summers of 1998 and 1999 brought me face-to-face with a lot of pain, more than I had ever dealt with before. At times, it prevented me from doing some of the things I wanted to. Other times, it interfered with doing things we do in our everyday lives. Some things were not as enjoyable as they could have been.

My first summer in Alaska, in 1998, I rebelled against my medication. I decided not to take my Methotrexate shots anymore. I had not seen a doctor or had any lab work done all that summer. I pretended the situation with my disease didn't even exist, and that I didn't have anyone to answer to.

I wanted to see what things would be like for me without all the drugs. Somehow I thought that it might help and that I would find myself feeling better without all the chemicals added to my body. By the end of the summer I had completely stopped taking the shots. I couldn't do them anymore. It was like a mental block, and I simply couldn't administer the shot to myself anymore.

On my trip back to Colorado, I stopped my Zorprin as well. I knew I didn't have enough to get me back home and decided not to make an effort to call and get more. I would let it run out and see how I felt. I wanted to keep my journal going specifically for such a time period to record what I was feeling and what was happening to my body.

It had been years since I first began a life of dependency on drugs, and never before had I considered what was actually going on with myself. Lots of feelings and I suppose most importantly pain had been superficially masked by drugs since my first doctor's visit.

Whatever the reason, I simply stopped taking medicine except for Advil in the morning and at night to help take the edge off. I anticipated a lot more pain, but questioned whether the Zorprin was even working. Apparently it was not doing much. Perhaps, I reasoned, the pain I was suffering already was due to the fact that my medication wasn't even working properly.

My mornings began being confronted with three trigger fingers—my two middle (third) fingers, and my right index finger. My neck was so stiff I couldn't touch my chin to my chest, my sore shoulders wouldn't allow me to lift my arms over my head, and all sorts of other pain. Hot showers and Advil helped some, but it was basically my will that pulled me through somehow.

When I was a teenager, I can remember having a journal with a lock on it. I didn't write in it often, but it was always there when I needed it. During the year of 1998, I once again began writing in a journal. Sometimes weeks and even months went by without an entry. Every once in a while, I would write about my arthritis and its role in my life at the time. My entries about the subject had a tendency to be on days that were tough on me and therefore were sporadic, but each entry gives some insight into what I was going through.

In September of that year I began taking time to write more extensively about the things I was going through. I was writing about my disease during the time I was pulling myself off of all the medication I had been on for years. Some samples:

September 1998:

"It's bad right now; the worst it has ever been throughout its years so far. Last time I was at the doctor's, I was told my knees were being attacked. I know when I go again they're going to say my neck and shoulders are being attacked, too. I wonder, Why? What makes it be passive for so long and then become completely active and destructive? I got the life sucked out of me today. I had to wake up early to arrive at work by 7 a.m., but I was given permission to come in later. When I went to bed last night, I already had a good idea what today was going to be all about for me. Although I tossed and turned a lot in my sleep last night, I feel like I got adequate sleep. But I was dragging before I even attempted to begin this morning.

My first waking moments were filled with so much pain and frustration that I could not hold back the flow of tears. I sat up the best I could in bed and let myself cry. When you wake up to mornings like this again and again it begins to get discouraging. I feel like I've tolerated a couple of rough hours many times, but it is getting to the point that it's at least one bad morning a week with others getting a slow start as well.

"I awoke and cringed as I rolled over onto my side. My shoulders hurt really bad. I moved my arms around a little to jar them loose from their stiffened positions and realized that my hands and fingers were cramped, too. Three trigger fingers to be exact, and they never got better throughout the day. A simple turn of my head took a great deal of effort, way more than usual and my knees weren't sure if they wanted to be bent or straightened. Either way, they ached.

"Needless to say, this is not how I like to start my day. After the tears were wiped away, I climbed down from my bunk to get ready for work. I realize it is going to take some extra time this morning. I struggle and wince putting my clothes on, bummed out that I don't have the time to take a nice hot shower that may at least help some.

"I complained to only two people that day—two friends who are aware of my arthritis and have a pretty good idea of what I'm going through. Of course, there is a lot more hidden that they are not aware of.

"I watch my hands become deformed. My fingers are starting to twist as arthritic joints do. They shake in the morning as I get out of bed. My neck is so stiff I need to turn my whole body to focus on anything. I can't get my clothes on without fighting back the tears that have come to my eyes. I want so much for someone to reach out and let me know I am not alone. Someone to let me know that not every day of my life is going to begin with this miserable struggle. I feel so alone during these times. No one is around, no one understands, no one cares that for my first hours of the day I am in a cruel world."

My first written account of what happened to me was recorded on my road trip back from Alaska to Colorado. The trip was filled with camping out nearly the entire way down.

September 14, 1998

"The trip has been nothing but great. But also a good time to think through all that driving. I've been thinking about a lot of things. Right now my arthritis is on the forefront of my mind. I did not make any efforts this summer to be seen or even tested, and I stopped my shots altogether. The worst, however, is that I have let my Zorprin run out. Honestly, lately it hasn't even felt like it's been working. Every morning on this trip is filled with pain in my shoulders, hands, and wrists although I have been sleeping on the most comfortable setup ever and never getting chilled. Something certainly is not right with me. I'm beginning to realize that I need to do something about it, but until I get back to Colorado, I pray that I may withstand the pain."

September 28, 1998

"Been in a lot of pain these last few days. Maybe because I have things on my mind. The Advil is not cutting it, and my will to get through this weakens every day. My hands are in so much pain that I'm struggling hard to do routine things. I cannot lift stuff anymore, and it feels like my body is crumbling beneath me. I'm trying to be strong and carry on."

October 6, 1998

"The pain is much worse. My neck and shoulders are worthless. Completing the simplest task is incredibly difficult. I've got lots on my mind, but it's too painful to write."

October 9, 1998

"Yesterday was a fallout day for me. I crashed to the bottom. I hurt so badly that I snapped and completely lost myself. I was shaky that I couldn't accomplish a thing. Everything I ate went right through me. I was inconsolable. I could not stop crying. I was miserable and scared. My house was too far away. I made my way to a friend's house to lie down. I cried myself to sleep, mentally and emotionally exhausted. Seven more days to make it until the doctor's. I hope I like him and that I can try something new. I'm damaging myself. I can feel it all over. My hands can barely hold this pen."

October 18, 1998

"It's been a painful week. My mind was cluttered. I went to the doctor and am on some new medication. A great visit. I have never wanted to go more or been happier with a visit to a rheumatologist. I already feel on hundred percent better in mind, body, and spirit. I guess I didn't realize how much the pain was eating away at me.

I still have a lot in my head, but things are becoming clearer. I was beginning to lose track of my own self, caught in a world where I knew I wouldn't survive. I wonder what my life would have been like years ago without modern medicine."

February 24, 1999

"I told someone yesterday that today was going to be a four star day. Unfortunately, things haven't exactly gone the way I'd hoped.

I went to my doctor's appointment feeling pretty good with the way things have been going. But he had a different opinion. According to him, I may "feel good," but I don't know what feeling good is like. So it's a switch to yet another new medication. Two shots per week, and a cost beyond my budget's reach.

The new medication is definitely worth trying, but it has stirred a mixture of old emotions. I'm frustrated *again* and when I call my mom all I can do is cry. I'm bummed out but know this is for the best. I just want something to work, something even remotely helping me restore my hope and courage to battle my aches and pains. I want the fatigue to go away. Help me understand what's happening to me and why."

12

More Drugs and More Shots

My experiment that summer was doing everything I wasn't supposed to do. As a result, I anticipated being reprimanded for this by my new doctor in Denver at my first appointment back from Alaska. I wasn't. When I met this doctor for the first time, I told him what I was feeling and how and why I had decided to stop my medications. In a way, I think he sympathized and had somewhat of an idea of why I did what I did.

All the other doctors have been great too, extremely reputable, but Dr. Bray and I made a connection stronger than any I had ever made before.

He put me on new medication right away—an anti-inflammatory called Naprolean® and a drug new on the market called Arava®. Both were oral, so no shots for a while. When my body did not respond positively to the Arava, more shots.

A few short months later, after having started Arava, I was approached by Dr. Bray about another new and improved drug on the market called Enbrel® (etanercept). Extremely new and expensive, this drug was supposed to reduce signs and symptoms of moderately to severe active rheumatoid arthritis. Not only was it to put the disease into remission, but to stop the damaging of joints along the way, reduce the pain and swelling, and therefore bring me immediate signs of improvement.

The drawback to this drug, aside from its outrageous price, was that it was administered through injections. Dr. Bray was aware of my feelings about shots and approached the manner delicately. I was ready to try anything, anything that would work. I had been going through so much pain I was ready to try this new wonder drug and see results.

So I began shots again, only this time it was twice a week. If it weren't for my parents, I couldn't have afforded it. Because of the way the drug is produced, by human cells, the cost was up around $2,100 for a month's supply. Fortunately, my co-pay was only $200, but even that was a lot of money for me to budget on my own.

Aside from having to be very careful about mixing the ingredients and storing the medication properly, the injections themselves were a piece of cake. The shots were subcutaneous, meaning they can go anywhere. There was no pain like before, and the process was simple. It was not my favorite thing to do, but since I hadn't a choice, I made the best of giving myself shots.

I often think about diabetics and the insulin shots they are required to take. It's part of their life. Now shots were part of mine. A nurse I worked with helped me a few times, injecting my arms to give my legs a break. I couldn't do my stomach because there wasn't enough tissue there to inject.

The first few shots went by without incident and then about the fourth, my leg broke out into a hives around the injection site and it itched like crazy. This was the only, and from what I understood, the most common side effect of the drug. Hydrocortisone cream helped keep the itching down and after about two or three months the hives happened a lot less frequently, grew smaller and smaller, usually only lasting a day or two. More often than not too, I would end up with a bruise at the injection site.

When positive results were not apparent after the first few months on Enbrel, I was put back on oral Methotrexate as well. Supposedly, the combination of the two drugs could be quite successful. And so I was back to three orally a week. I tried to keep my hopes up, my chin up, and my head high. I wanted to know when I was going to feel better.

In spring of 1999, my neck and shoulders stiffened so badly that I had to turn my whole body instead of just my neck, which would shake with weakness and pain when I tried to move it. I called Dr. Bray begging for a referral to meet with a physical therapist to help me. For the next two months I saw a physical therapist. She helped me tremendously and restored my hope. I had stretching exercises to do. I had strengthening exercises to do. And with every appointment, I felt better.

The summer of 1999 brought me back to my hometown of Southboro, Massachusetts, to work at the same camp I had worked at before I moved out West. I also wanted to spend some time with my family. The humidity back East brought me nothing but pain. I felt like I hadn't even spent time with a physical therapist. Every single morning my neck screamed with pain. I continued with the exercises I was given, but to no avail. I tried heating pads, my trusty bag of rice, my neck roll for sleeping, but nothing lessened the pain I felt.

I had no choice, but to grin and bear it and hope that when I arrived back in Colorado my doctor would have some suggestions for me. I drove to Colorado the last week in September, sleeping three nights in the back of my jeep on a bed I'd made with both the fiber mattress and my new feather bed as well. For having to sleep in the car, it was comfortable.

When I finally saw my doctor in Denver, he wasn't pleased with how I was doing and increased the dose of Methotrexate—the drug that gives me stomach trouble. My frustration skyrocketed. How many times was my medication going to be changed? Increased? How long would it take? I began seriously thinking about seeking other forms of healing. I was ready to spend the money and make an effort to try an acupuncturist and even try Chinese herbal remedies. Anything!

I called around to a few names I had heard of and finally set up my first appointment to try the needles. I was quite used to being stuck by now. It was absolutely amazing. I couldn't put into words how acupuncture made me feel. I lay there on the table with about 26 needles stuck in me, an infrared lamp to help with extra soreness in my elbows, and uncontrollable tears falling from my eyes. I could feel something happening to me. I wasn't sure what, but I felt it.

I asked a lot of questions and learned that the whole premise behind acupuncture and the needles was to release blocks of energy that flow though your body that cause the pain and stress your body suffers. I could almost feel this happening. I was given specific herbs to take to help with various symptoms I was experiencing—some for inflammation, some for immunity. The first pills I actually couldn't wait to swallow. They were a lot, but eventually I was supposed to be feeling better enough to reduce my other medications and even the herbs themselves.

I saw my acupuncturist once a week for the first month and then every other week. Later on it was once a month. I could feel things work through my body. The natural herbs were doing great things for me. My acupuncturist genuinely cared about me and what was happening. She had success stories about other patients she had treated and was still treating with my type of arthritis.

My third visit to her marked the last dose I had for the Enbrel shots. The last batch that I took had some pretty dull needles in them, and I didn't want to do them anymore. I was to call my doctor when this dose ended to discuss options if I didn't feel a difference. I hadn't felt a difference in years. So, I switched yet again. This time back to Arava to try that combination with the Methotrexate. I was told that with patients where the Enbrel/Methotrexate combination hasn't worked, the Arava/Methotrexate combination had sometimes been successful.

I am always willing to try something out. Unfortunately, the transition period between when the time that I stopped the Enbrel and the time the Arava finally was in my system was rough for me. I ached all over. The only thing I looked forward to were my acupuncture appointments. They helped me tremendously even if it was for only a day or two.

Those needles work! I will continue to go to these appointments and take my herbs and other medication, because I know something is going to work for me. It has to!

13

Falling Apart

Often I get a dreadful feeling that I am literally falling apart. I feel that my body is slowly giving up on me, even through times when I am willing with all my might for it to hang in there for me. My disease began as a slow progression and has gradually seemed to hit the hyper-drive speed.

What's scary is that I only see the damage on the surface, and x-rays can only reveal the carnage on the inside. First wrists, hands, feet, and then knees and hips, which were bad for a period of about two months or so, and then were OK again—almost like someone had turned a switch on and then turned it off again.

X-rays show permanent damage to my knees. Now it has been hanging around my shoulders and neck. Every day I wake up with aches that last most of the mornings. The pain never really goes away, but as my day starts I try to push it far from my mind. It is an impossible task at times. I have to turn my whole body to look at things, as if my head and body were one unit, with my neck fusing the two together. There are times when it is impossible to stop the tears of pain. My will is strong, but the tears are like those that fall when peeling an onion, and I can't get them to stop.

I frequently walk around wondering when the rest of my joints will begin to fail me. The day my elbows wouldn't straighten I was astounded. Three new nodules on my elbows and neck crushed my hopes for recovery. I was falling apart. Sometimes I feel the sooner the better. I might as well get this over with. Nothing seems to help anyway. Doesn't matter how much or what medication I take. My physical world is wrecked and always will be. My mental state and strength must stay strong just to get me to the next day.

My mind is on a roller coaster. I know I need to be strong, I can fight this, I can beat it, eat right, keep exercising, stay fit. . . I'm worthless, I can't do this, it's killing me, I can't stay in shape. I'm falling apart.

14

Future

Countless times I think of my future, a natural response in all of us. Not only do I think about what I'm doing with my life and what I want my goals and accomplishments to be, but also about my health. Perhaps I think about this more often because I feel it is something that I don't seem to have much control over.

Every day I make a conscious effort to watch the foods I eat, and there are times when I'm good about staying in shape as well. Then there are the things that I can't control. When I'm having bad days, I think about being only 27 years old and it's this bad. I know it is only going to get worse as I get older—unless, of course, it goes into remission. But how long can I continue to rekindle the flame of hope? It's hard to fathom the idea of remission when I don't have any sign of improvement.

I think about a husband who might not have the patience to help me cope. I think about my own children that I might not be able to pick up and hold. Sometimes I see myself living my life alone. And sometimes I imagine that I was destined to live a short life. Maybe that is why I don't plan ahead. I have goals I want to reach, but I cannot sit down and plan for a future that seems so uncertain to me.

Maybe someone will find a cure for rheumatoid arthritis that will end this misery for once and all. I hope so. Or perhaps at that point I will already be crippled beyond repair. I get scared. It's like a bad nightmare that you cannot wake up from. I can't stop thinking about it. What's going to happen to me? Does my fate have a good ending or am I destined to take it to my grave? Doesn't everything happen for a reason? Then what's the reason?

Do I pray? Should I pray? I was raised Roman Catholic, was baptized, even confirmed. However, since my days of having to go to church every Sunday morning for services I never completely understood, I have stopped going to church. I still believe in a God, but I am unsure what religious following to believe in. I just know that there are a lot of things that the Catholic religion follows that I don't.

I have been told that if I practice faith and religion, pray and devote myself to God, that will help my situation. I can't pray for myself—not when there are millions of others out in the world suffering far more than I ever will. Such a prayer would be selfish. What was meant to happen to me will happen. That is my fate and destiny.

I tried Yoga and a degree of meditation for a short period of time. My brother David was the influence there. Some of the stretches became difficult because I was always stiff. I was easily discouraged and lacked the motivation to continue trying for any length of time.

The only thing that feels good to me when I'm stiff in the morning is a hot shower. Not until I begin to loosen up a few hours into the day am I able to stretch and exercise. But no sooner do I stop the exercise and the stiffness creeps its way back in. Little by little, I have been getting into more of a routine.

15

Perspective

Some people live their life without ever putting what they do or what they have or who they are in perspective. Others undergo events in their lives that change their perspective dramatically. In my own experience, many incidents have given me the opportunity to appreciate what my life is all about.

It may sound strange, but when you are up against a struggle or battle, you act like a fight-or-flight animal, which is what the human species is. You can choose to give up and painfully serve out your loss, or you can choose to hang in there fighting to the bitter end. Live your life for what it is. Never let anything come in the way of doing what you want to do with your life. Just do it wisely.

When I was first diagnosed with JRA, I did not accept it. I did not know what putting things in perspective meant. When I was twenty years old and was involved in the car accident, I painfully accepted what had happened and did understanding something of what having a perspective was. I still think there was a certain amount of adolescence influencing my mind at that time, but I thought long and hard about why it happened and what it was all supposed to mean in my life. It occurred for a reason, but what? It was to make me stronger, but why?

After the accident I began to accept my chronic illness and what was physically going on in my body. I began to put many things in perspective. I learned what was important to me and started building my belief that everything in our lives happens for a reason. Although the reason may not always be clear to me, I have a better understanding and acceptance.

Within the last few years, I have come to appreciate the positive role that rheumatoid arthritis plays in my life. There are still times that I try to forget it's there and perhaps don't take care of myself the way I should, but the pain brings me back to the reality of it all.

I know what I want. I want a loving husband to share a family with, my own house with some dogs, my cat of course and maybe some horses. I want to teach children for a good chunk of years, and then, perhaps save up enough to open and own a preschool. I want to grow old, but I don't want to grow old with RA. Sometimes it feels like the disease will take me down to the bitter end. Crippling at only age twenty-seven, I don't even want to imagine what state I may be in fifty years from now.

My friends and family are very dear to me, and I want to spend the time I can with them—not because I feel time running out, but because I can. Too many people who touch our daily lives slip into and out of our scope. There's nothing stopping you from holding onto those memories. You just have to remind yourself, "Do it because you can." Don't let time slip by you so that you may regret it in years to come. Trust what is in your heart to lead you to your next step in life no matter what changes or directions it may lead you through.

A couple of years ago I wrote a song. It had meaning to it and I did it because I could and I wanted to. Eventually my beloved brother helped to put together a rough recording of it. Here are the words to that song:

"GIVE INTO YOUR SOUL"

Late at night when sleep's no friend
And a thousand thoughts prevail.
Every thought brings a brand new dream.
Let your mind slip into that world.

CHORUS:

Give into your soul, let your spirit reign,
It will take miles away.
And though you think that you've been there
    before
It will never ever be the same.

Take the time you need to learn about yourself,
Never knowing what's ahead of you.
Get on with your life before it passes you by
Hold onto happiness forever.

Times may pass and things will change.
Accept them for what they are.
Changes are the steps to the fate you possess
Step up and follow your path.

CHORUS

Toss away your fears and learn how to live.
Learn to take it all in stride.
Things were meant to be so except them as they
    are.
Get up and go live your life.

CHORUS

16

The Last Hopeful

It's interesting how life fits so perfectly with the analogy of a roller coaster ride. There are times that are so exciting, you can hardly hear yourself breathe. And other times all that excitement scares away. A roller coaster has its ups and downs. So do our lives. However, in your typical amusement ride, there are a set number of rises and falls. The ride is over in a matter of minutes, even though we sometimes wish for it to continue.

It's never over in life. The ride continues even though sometimes we wish it to be through. And there isn't a set amount of "ups and downs" for us all. Our life ride is completely unique to the individual. Maybe there will be more ups than downs, more falls than rises or maybe there will be a balance between the two. Some rises are bigger than others, and some falls take us to a place where we may think it's impossible to go up again.

I don't feel like my life ride has been that much different from the experience of others. I have enjoyed some great highs throughout my life and some terrible lows, too. My medications have created a ride of their own for me.

Now they're working, now they're not. I experience side effects. I am hopeful for a new drug to help, and have hoped so for every drug I have tried. Every new medication I have placed my hopes in, has failed me thus far.

In the last months before the new millennium, I was put on the last drug available for me to try. The last hopeful if you will. The Arava I had been taking left me with a body rash and stomach problems that stayed with me for over a month. Because of Arava's long half life, it took a while to flush it entirely out of my system. I lost my appetite and what I managed to get into my system ended coming right back out. I lost weight and became extremely weak and tired.

At that time, Remicade® had been approved by the FDA for less than a month to treat rheumatoid arthritis. The cost was unbelievable—over $5,000 for one dose. Amazingly, it was covered under my insurance. The treatment was intravenous and had to be done at a hospital. It was three treatments within the first six weeks and then every other month after that.

I experienced a mixture of feelings as I sat there in the medical center in Breckenridge for my first dose. The medication is administered over the course of two hours. My good friend Marie hung out with me and lent her support. The time went by relatively quickly with her there. and we made light of the situation. We laughed a lot, and this enabled me not to think about the significance this "new" drug may have on my life.

I went home that night feeling a little strange. Not bad, but different. Since Remicade was new to the arthritis world, I had done my own research about it through the internet. I learned that it had been prescribed for the past two years to treat Crone's disease, which involves the bowel system. Although most of the explanation I found was written in scientific terms, which are foreign to me, I was able to decipher the gist of it. My highest concern was knowing what the side effects were. After all, every drug I had tried in the past, ended at this point. There didn't seem to be anything major there, and I skimmed over a page that talked about infections.

My first two treatments went by without a hitch. I desperately tried to feel differently, but it was hard to tell where to pinpoint my current state of well being. Was I feeling better because my rash had finally dissipated, and I had gained back an appetite? Or was it this drug, my "last hopeful"? I became sick between my second and third treatments with infections of every sort.

I had almost anticipated it. For the time being, I feel that Remicade is the last hope for me to fight my rheumatoid arthritis into remission. I can't help but throw all my hopes and dreams into this liquid dripping into my veins. What else can I do?

Right now I'm on the up side of the roller coaster, at the point where you are so excited and anxious to be on the upside, but yet so scared to feel what it may be like going down the other side.

When I went back for my third treatment, I was feeling fairly good—at least compared to way I'd felt the past several months of my life. And then something went wrong, terribly wrong. As I lay there waiting to have the IV set up, an incredible feeling of discomfort came over me. For no particular reason that I could tell, I began to develop a lump in my throat and could tell that things were not going to work out as planned. Altogether, two nurses stuck me five times unable to thread a vein and on the last try when they thought they had it, they were mistaken. The injection infiltrated, and my arm filled up with fluid. With every attempt they made, my anxiety level grew higher and higher until the lump in my throat finally gave way to my tears. I was trying hard to hang tough, but when

I saw my arm begin to bubble and felt the pain that accompanied it, I cried.

That was it. I was told that I should come back another day when the more experienced nurses were working. I left in despair, feeling defeated in a way. Is this what I was going to have to go through every time?

I don't know why I cried so much that day. What is it that makes us cry anyway? Confusion, frustration, anger, joy, happiness, loss, fear. Maybe we cry sometimes because we simply need it. But I cried a lot. And my fears, frustration, and confusion were once again restored and brought to the forefront.

I understand having problems. It's when you have problems on top of other problems and still on top of others that put me on the edge. On that roller coaster ride again, and all I want to do is get off the damned thing because it's making me sick with fear.

When I returned two days later for a second attempt at medication, I was more nervous than at any other time in my arthritic career. Everyone could tell. They all remembered that I was the one who had been stuck unsuccessfully. I took a deep breath as the needle dived through my skin once again. To my surprise, this time it worked.

I closed my eyes to put that other dark day behind me. I thought a lot that session. I was told that my veins were difficult due to all the Methotrexate in my system. A central injection line was suggested to eliminate the misery I might continually experience. My thoughts were filled with my day, just that one day and how I had lived my life in it. What began as a day of emptiness and fear, slowly turned into one of hope for the future.

I went back to my doctor only to be told that I still wasn't doing well—something I obviously already knew. Long story short, I was put on a higher dosage of Remicade and prescribed Prednisone on a regular basis. I had been on Prednisone, a steroid, in the past to help with flare-ups, but only on a temporary basis.

Prednisone makes me eat like a horse and sends my mind into a thinking frenzy. I had trouble relaxing and never really had a clear head. So after a few weeks, I stopped taking it.

I continued my life for the next few months with the "last hopeful" in the back of my mind. But the combination of my germ-infested work environment and the fact that my immunity system seems to be on a extended vacation, got me sick again. Really sick!

I had a few friends in town visiting, and it happened to be my birthday as well—the one night out of the year that I am not very cautious about my alcohol consumption. This year, despite the number of shots I drank, I managed to remain relatively coherent throughout the evening. I'd had a terrific day so far. A bunch of friends and I had hit the Collegiate range of 14,000 foot mountains in Buena Vista, Colorado, to go horse back riding. Four hours in the saddle with the added entertainment of my good friend Mike on the back of his trusty stead Cool Cat (aka "CC"). Mike had "the look,"—a stylish country western thrift store shirt with a hat shaped only for him.

For dinner that night. . .sushi. I have never eaten that much sushi in my entire life. And saki, of course. I was intelligent enough to pace myself with that. It was so nice to be with so many friends that I knew cared about me. And it was wonderful to see everyone having a good time. This is the way celebrations should be. So of course, after dinner, to a bar for some drinking, dancing, and great conversations about life.

Over the course of the next few days, I began developing pain in my lower back, something I had never experienced before. I had signs of getting a head cold and started to feel tired and run down. I figured I was coming down with something *again.* The pain in my back persisted until I was driven to tears.

I was in so much pain that I decided I needed a massage, some acupuncture—something. I suffered for a few days until I developed a fever and began vomiting everything I drank. I wasn't eating anything and had lost my appetite. A visit to the emergency room, a few x-rays and a couple of IV bags later, I was told I had pneumonia. That knocked the socks right off of me. I became depressed, had no energy, no appetite, and got to thinking about this germ battlefield I work in. It is so aggravating when you're sick. And it's depressing when you fight infection after infection and never feel like you're getting better or that you're ever healthy.

I try so hard to take care of myself with plenty of rest, good food, exercise. But my efforts are continually thwarted by my intolerance to lingering germs. It all shines back on my disease, my lack of a strong immune system, and my apparent inability to be in control of it all.

There isn't a day that goes by when I don't think about my life with RA. Sometimes in my sleep, I dream about it. But I hold my head high every day and keep my mind clear of what may happen. I'll go to play tennis one afternoon and feel great. Every volley with the tennis ball has me feeling stronger and stronger. "Is that my will or are things really working here for me?" I think to myself. Mornings I'll wake up and my hands are stiff with that ol' trigger finger that used to bug me. Am I sore from sleeping badly, or am I starting towards the low end of the roller coaster again? It's hard to tell. But it's OK to go on. Go on believing that it will work, because it may. And if it doesn't, have faith that by then something new and great will have come along.

I leave you, not knowing what my future may hold. But I can tell you how I will live my life. Through my ups and downs, I will live life to the fullest. I will take each day as it comes with a grain of salt. I will do my best to take care of myself, by eating right, keeping up with exercise, getting the rest I need, and staying happy. When I need help, I'll ask for it. And when I have the opportunity to lend a hand to help someone else, I will, wholeheartedly. Whether or not I am ever able to put this disease into remission, I will have won.

17

A Normal Life

I lead a normal life. It is normal to me. I have done the things I have wanted to do and have plans to do what I haven't done. I have been making memories every step along my way. Here's to it being only a fraction of what is still to come for me.

My heart reaches out to those who share the pain of this world. It is a battle we will win with our powerful hearts and souls. We will prevail even if we appear to fail.

Get up and go live your life.

THE END